The M.O. Scale

Know and Control Your Future

James R. Samuels, Ph.D.
&
Jay Klusky, Ph.D.

U   E
P T O N
Press
Portland, Oregon

The M.O. Scale:
Know and Control Your Future

by
James R. Samuels, Ph.D. &
Jay Klusky, Ph.D.

Published by:
Uptone Press
7689 SW 74th Ave. #3
Portland, OR. 97223

Samuels, James R.
Klusky, Jay
The M.O. Scale: Know and Control Your Future

ISBN: 978-09634011-5-7
LCCN: 2010937464

$12.95 Paperback
Printed in the United States of America

This book is dedicated to

Jack Horner
philosopher, teacher, friend

Founder of Eductivism and
The Personal Creative Freedoms Foundation

His work continues through the unbroken chain of students and
teachers he inspired.

The M.O. Scale

Know and Control
Your Future

Table of Contents

Introduction

Student and Teacher

The year was 1974. I was a sophomore in college on the east coast, majoring in music theory and experiencing my first mid-life crisis. You see I didn't have much of an ear, was not a very good clarinetist, and could not sing worth a darn. Now for the first time I was really taking a hard look at my future and I was fairly certain I was on the wrong path. It was then that a graduate student with whom I had been working told me about his summer vacation. He had taken classes in applied philosophy from a gentleman out in Portland, Oregon. The description of his studies piqued my curiosity.

A few weeks later I wrote Dr. Samuels explaining my situation and he invited me out to Oregon at the end of the school year. So in May, with $300 and a duffel bag, I went to Portland for the summer. I was so interested in Dr. Samuels' work that with the exception of my 3 1/2 year hiatus at UCLA to do my graduate work, I have been in Portland studying and working with him ever since. During the course of our relationship he has been my teacher and mentor, colleague and friend. I could not have asked for better.

In the mid-1970s, he began working on the M.O. Scale and introduced it in 1976. The more I worked to apply it, the greater appreciation I had for its potential. During the course of my studies in psychology I, of course, came across a number of other seemingly similar constructs; most of them taking the form of personality inventories, the Myers-Briggs being the most widely known. Most of these view personality as a set of fixed characteristics and so work to define various typologies.

The M.O. Scale construct is different. It eschews the concept of permanent personality and focuses instead on providing a lens for understanding why people do what they do and get the results they get. Moreover, with this understanding the Scale becomes both a predictive and prescriptive tool pointing the way towards helping people change the way they interact with the world and so increase their chances of success.

It has now been 20 years since receiving my Ph.D. in cognitive psychology and the M.O. Scale continues to be one of the most useful and reliable tools I have to guide me in my professional and personal interactions. Understand the M.O. Scale and practice applying it and it will likely serve you as well as it has served me.

Jay Klusky

In 1962, I learned a memory technique from a book written by Harry Lorayne. I immediately went out into our living room and asked my father and aunt Pat to write down a numbered list of twelve items randomly chosen from around the room. They did this aloud, so I could hear the list being made. To their amazement, and mine, I was able to name each item when given its number and the number of each item when asked – all from memory after hearing it just the one time. The advantage this has given me over my lifetime simply cannot be measured.

This event started me on a lifetime quest of discovering what other abilities we humans have sitting in our minds, waiting to be discovered and awakened.

The M.O. Scale provides a framework that can awaken in you an awareness of what is governing your fundamental behavior and that of the people surrounding you. This knowledge can change the way you see the world and bring you a whole new level of success in everything you do.

More, it can bring you new choices in the way you interact with people; choices most people don't know exist. Work hard and enjoy.

Jim Samuels

Getting the Most from the Book

While the book is short page-wise, people have found it pretty thick conceptually. There is much specialized vocabulary and sometimes simple thoughts have deeper meaning than one might realize at first glance. So take your time. The Scale itself is presented on page 16 in the second chapter. It will help to refer to it often as you read until you are familiar with it. Have fun.

Chapter I

Peering into the Future: Chance or Choice?

Peering into the Future

Have you ever been surprised by someone? Have you ever been in a relationship that was seemingly going well, when out of the blue your partner informed you that they are leaving? Have you ever employed someone who was a standup, reliable worker - until the day you found out he had been stealing from the company for the past two years? Have you ever been shocked to find out your son or daughter wasn't the happy kid you thought they were?

Life is full of surprises. Some of these surprises are fun: birthday parties for example. Some surprises deeply move you, like when the person you love asks you to marry them. Many surprises are relatively inconsequential. However, there are some surprises, like the ones above, that can put us at great disadvantage, cause us much pain, and significantly impact our lives.

At times in hindsight we can see some of the clues that we missed. More often than not though, these events catch us totally off guard, and when we look back upon them it is hard for us to see how we could have known. In an effort to make sense of them we conclude it was the Divine's will, karma, or just bad luck.

Not only could you have known, in many cases you could likely have changed the outcome. In fact, the clues were always present for all to see. You just needed to know what you were looking for. Drop a city boy into the Kalahari Desert and he will die of thirst within days, yet the San people, who have lived there for millennia see signs of water all around.

Look through the lens of the M.O. Scale and you will see the clues. See the clues and you will be able to turn events to your advantage and the advantage of most, if not all the parties involved. Look through the lens of the M.O. Scale and you will be able to develop the foresight and wisdom to identify the best people to have around you; those who would make the best friends, employees, business associates, and life-partners.

Chance or Choice?

Have you ever wondered why some people fail consistently while others succeed? Why one person is miserable and another who leads a similar life with similar circumstances is happy? Why some people are seemingly star-crossed while others seem to have fate smile upon them?

Have you ever thought about why someone you know habitually shoots themselves in the foot when it comes to romance, yet at the same time has great success in business? Have you wondered why some people have such a hard time getting their act together while others have had their act together all their lives? Ever thought about your own situations; why it is you do not do well in some areas of your life and do quite well in others?

When people think about these questions those who consider themselves to be unsuccessful will likely attribute this to factors outside of the individual's control: parenting, educational opportunities, socioeconomic status. Those who consider themselves successful will likely chalk this up to factors within the individual's control: focus, ingenuity, hard work.

Of course both are true. But why will one person focus when another will not? Why will one person choose to be disciplined when another chooses to remain on their couch? Why will one person give up while another keeps plugging away? The answers have much to do with a person's outlook, their approach to the world. Approach the desert as a land filled with danger and you will respond one way; approach it as a land of opportunity and you will respond very differently.

Our approaches to the world are strongly influenced by our parenting, friendships, socio-economic status, and environment. More specifically, our approaches develop as a result of our past experiences of stress and success. We develop them as we grow and by and large we remain unconscious of them. So these most important aspects of our lives, how we see the world and respond to it are, for the most part, simply a function of chance and circumstance. This does not have to be the case.

Yes, there is a fair amount of randomness in the universe - stuff happens. There are a number of factors impacting our lives that are out of our control. However, how we approach our lives and how we respond to events are not among them. These can be largely within our power. We can choose how we perceive events, what we think about them, and how we respond to them.

Where one person sees being fired from their job as a tragedy, experiences it as a great loss, traumatizing them for months or even years; another person will, after the initial shock wears off, see the same event as an opportunity to go into business for themselves and begin a new phase of their life. Where one person views a heart attack as the beginning of the end; another will view it as a wake-up call. We all have choices; that is if we are aware of them and if we have the ability to act upon them.

Understand the M.O. Scale and you will gain the capacity to develop the ability to choose how we will approach and respond to the world. Change your approach and you will fundamentally change the way you respond to, and experience, life. So the question for us all becomes: will we leave our lives to chance or will we develop our capacity to choose?

Chapter 2

Introducing the M.O. Scale

What is an M.O.?

So, what is an M.O.? An M.O. is an unconscious Method of Operation; an unknown approach to engaging with the world. M.O.s act as lenses through which we perceive and interpret those perceptions, make decisions and draw conclusions. It can not be over emphasized: M.O.s are so influential that they can dominate and rule our lives.

All approaches are not equal. Some approaches work better than others. Like landing an airplane, if the angle of approach is too flat, the plane will miss the runway; to steep and the plane will most certainly crash. There are angles of approach a pilot must take to land the plane safely. Similarly, there are approaches to every aspect of our lives that will greatly decrease or increase our chances of success.

Just as all approaches are not created equal, neither are all lenses. Some lenses are more occluded, distorted than others, while some are much more clear and provide a more accurate picture of what is actually happening around us. It is more difficult for a person who sees the glass as half empty to be happy and fulfilled than it is for the person who sees the glass as half full.

There are twelve M.O.s. Each is comprised of three components: an attitude, an emotion, and a behavior. These all operate in conjunction with each other to make up a given Method of Operation. The attitudinal component names the M.O. It describes a particular approach to the world, a particular lens. The emotional component describes the emotion that is connected with the particular attitude. The behavioral component describes the behavior manifested when a person is expressing through a particular attitude. The twelve M.O.s are arranged in a scale that delineates each M.O. and its relationship to the others.

More than a scale of approaches and lenses, the M.O. Scale is also a scale of motivations. Each M.O. describes what people are motivated by. Some people are motivated by fear; they will act under a perceived threat, real or imagined. These are often the people who insist that they work best "under pressure." Other people won't go into action until someone or something, real or imagined, ticks them off enough – then watch out! Still others are motivated by the joy of success and the pursuit of happiness; when they see an opportunity to improve their situation they jump on it.

The M.O. Scale also describes what people are motivated to do. Believe it or not some people actually are motivated to fail, they are actually working to create situations in which loss is the most likely outcome. Some people are motivated to undermine the people they work with and the projects they work on. There are those who are motivated to seek challenges they can overcome, and others to create opportunities to conserve their resources.

For the most part our actual motivations lay below our awareness. Ask a person who is making mistakes if they are doing so on purpose and they will likely say they are not. Yet if you observe them, you will watch them making those same mistakes over and over again. We've all witnessed a friend or family member do this. Many of us have attempted to point this out to them and have been dumb-founded when they just do not see it and keep on doing what they have been doing. This is, in fact, their M.O. at work.

The M.O. Scale is a very powerful construct. Understand the M.O. Scale and you will understand why people do what they do. Understand the M.O. Scale and you will gain great insight into what people will do next. Understand the M.O. Scale and you will be more able to influence the direction of your interactions. Understand the M.O. Scale and you will more fully appreciate your own motivations. Perhaps of greatest import, understand the M.O. Scale and you can learn how to choose methods of operation that will give you the greatest chance to succeed at being, doing, and having what you want.

So without further ado . . .

The M.O. Scale (Dr. James Samuels)

	M.O./Attitude	Emotion	Behavior
Goal-Oriented ▲	+6 Confident	Certainty	Knows
	+5 Conservative	Contentment	Maintains
	+4 Successful	Happiness	Wins
	+3 Interested	Curiosity	Focuses
	+2 Careless	Boredom	Unfocuses
	+1 Determined	Anger	Strikes out (for)
Problem-Oriented ▼	-1 Rebelling	Anger	Strikes out (against)
	-2 Undermining	Resentment	Destabilizes
	-3 Failing	Fear	Causes Losing
	-4 Failed	Grief	Causes Loss
	-5 Defeated	Apathy	No Desires
	-6 Lifeless	Hopelessness	No Future

The scale has two halves. The line in the middle separates the lower problem-oriented M.O.s from the upper goal-oriented M.O.s. Problem-oriented M.O.s focus on addressing undesirable conditions. Problem-oriented M.O.s are based on the intention to retreat from a condition considered to be negative. Generally speaking, pessimists are those who approach the world from this lower half of the scale.

Goal-oriented M.O.s focus on the attainment of something desirable, be it a state or material object. These M.O.s are based on the intention to reach for a condition considered to be positive. Generally speaking, optimists are those who approach the world from this upper half of the scale.

The arrows indicate decreasing and increasing functionality and likelihood of success. So, a person operating from -3, *Failing* is less likely to be successful than a person operating from +3, *Interested.* Before we describe how it all works, we'll explain each M.O. We'll start with the problem-oriented M.O.s then move on to the goal-oriented M.O.s. This way we can finish on a more positive note.

Rebelling: -1

Those operating from the *Rebelling* M.O. often find the world a place of struggle, of problems, of people and things that get in their way. The signature emotion of the *Rebelling* M.O. is anger; the signature behavior: striking out against. Conflict, both physical and verbal, is common. People who are *Rebelling* seem to be more interested in resisting than building up. They can be anti-tax, anti-government, anti-business, anti-religion, or anti-smoking; you get the picture.

Undermining: -2

Those operating from the *Undermining* M.O. lack the courage to address the world directly. They believe they have to hide their true goals and intentions. Remember the bully in school? You know, the kid who used to pick on people and get in a lot of fights? The bully was operating from the *Rebelling* M.O.

Now there was also the one on whom the bully picked, the pickee. He wanted to stand up for himself but was too scared to face his nemesis. Sometimes this kid went home and took his frustration out on his younger sister. Sometimes this kid found a way to sneak behind the bully's back and get him in trouble. These kinds of solutions are typical of the *Undermining* M.O.

The signature emotion of **Undermining** is resentment, the signature behavior: destabilization. Underminers tend to be passive-aggressive. Too fearful to face things head on, they look for ways to take others down secretly. They are the ones who smile at and complement those who, minutes ago, they were criticizing behind their backs. They seem to take pleasure from others' misfortunes. Perhaps you know the type.

Failing: -3

Those operating from the M.O. of **Failing** move through the world as if it were a dangerous place. The signature emotion: fear. This is the M.O. of worriers; those who are afraid things won't work out. Behaviorally, they cause losing. **Failing** people will find a way to not be successful; though they won't quite go all the way and lose. **Failing** can be quite the balancing act. Those operating from **Failing** work it out so they remain in a state of almost having lost. For example, the person who says they have a goal of being a professional athlete, yet who does little to get themselves in truly athletic shape. They can remain in a state of failing for quite a long time yet never quite fail.

Failed: -4

People operating from the **Failed** M.O. expect to lose, expect things not to work out for them. And as a result of their expectation they become the prime cause of their failure. The student who expects to not be successful in school blows off an assignment or "accidentally" forgets to study for a test. The salesperson who spaces out an important meeting or doesn't leave himself enough time to prepare for an important presentation is the cause of his or her own failure. The signature emotion of the **Failed**

M.O. is grief: "It's sad. I already know how it's going to turn out, and it's not good."

Defeated: -5

When some people experience too much failure they give up; they become **Defeated**. They no longer have the motivation to engage. Operating from this M.O. people no longer have goals. A young man who time and again is shot down in his attempts at romance decides it's no longer worth the heartache and gives up even trying. The entrepreneur who fails in her attempts to start a number of businesses decides to "just get a boring job" and remains professionally unfulfilled. The signature emotion is apathy. "Why bother." "It's just not worth it."

Lifeless: -6

Lifeless is the M.O. people are operating from when they cannot even imagine a future for themselves. The signature emotion is hopelessness. If you have seen the blank face of a person who has truly given up all hope of even surviving, you have a good idea what people who are operating from this M.O. look like.

These are the problem-oriented M.O.s. As you can imagine, the lower down the scale one gets the harder it would be to succeed. Now let's explore the goal-oriented M.O.'s.

Determined: +1

Determined is the lowest M.O. from which success becomes probable. Similar to the **Rebelling** M.O. those operating from the M.O. of **Determined** also find the world a place of struggle. However, rather than viewing the world as something to fight *against*, they see the host of causes to fight *for*. People in this M.O. see the world full of challenges to be overcome so they can achieve their goals. Also similar to **Rebelling**, the signature emotion associated with **Determined** is anger. The key difference is that rather than direct their anger *against* something, **Determined** individuals direct it *towards* an accomplishment.

Determined people grit their teeth and fight on. No pain, no gain. People operating from this M.O. will tend to see problems where they do not necessarily exist. They then will solve these problems, creating more work than is necessary for themselves, and continue on until they finally, with much effort, achieve their goal.

Careless: +2

"What's this doing here? – you may ask. **Careless** is the M.O. that people may operate from when things are going well enough. After one has worked hard to stabilize a situation s/he may lose their focus and begin to make mistakes. The key here is that the situation has stabilized; things are going well enough. Through their determination, they have made progress on their goal and can relax (become careless.) The signature emotion of the **Careless** M.O. is boredom. We've all seen this and many of us have personal experience. We all know the person who was determined to get that raise, worked hard, finally got it, and then relaxed, dropped their attention and started slipping up. S/he then slipped up enough to put themselves under the gun again then worked their way out. They may continue to advance but rarely do they advance too far.

Interested: +3

To move beyond *Careless* one needs to maintain their focus, but without the anger of determined. This increased interest will often happen after a setback caused by some carelessness. Those operating from the M.O. of Interest find it natural and easy to put their attention on something and maintain their focus. If they maintain their focus on their goal, they will succeed. However, sometimes they can be so interested in an aspect of a project they are working on they may lose sight of the bigger picture. The signature emotion of the Interested M.O. is curiosity. Think of how naturally curious young children are; they are sponges soaking up the world around them. The *Interested* individual approaches the world with the same child-like wonder. They see the world as a fascinating place and bring their curiosity and focus to all their engagements with people, material objects, and ideas. Because of their heightened curiosity, these people tend to notice things the rest of us may miss.

Successful: +4

To be *Successful* a person needs to maintain their interest/focus all the way through to the accomplishment of their goal. Those operating from the *Successful* M.O. see opportunities for success all around them. They win, and they win on their own terms. The signature emotion is happiness. When we win on our own terms and are successful at something that is meaningful to us we are happy. Where the person operating from Interested easily focuses on people, things, and/or ideas, those operating from *Successful* maintain their focus on a key element – the goals they have set for themselves.

Conservative: +5

While successful people win consistently they may not necessarily hold on to their rewards. We have a friend who has made a lot of money in his life and has spent almost the same amount. Making money is easy for him; he is very successful at it. He is equally successful at spending it. To clarify further, imagine a person has decided they need 3 million dollars in assets to retire. They take many risks to attain their goal and reach it. If they are operating from Successful they might keep taking risks to expand their wealth. If they are operating from *Conservative* they will hold on to their $3 million and only risk money over and above their target.

Those operating from the *Conservative* M.O. hold onto what they have gained; they conserve their resources. Emotionally, they are content. They live within their means. Whether we are talking about time, energy, or material resources *Conservative* people always hold some in reserve. They maintain their wealth; that is, they maintain their successes. More, they tend to set goals that have ongoing, repeating returns.

Confident: +6

At the top of the M.O. scale is *Confident*. Those operating from this M.O. are certain of their power; they know what they are capable of and they know what they are not capable of. They know they will be successful and they know they will make things work. They are certain they can enter any situation and find the advantages.

Imagine a young singer-songwriter getting her first recording contract. She would be excited. She would likely be wildly happy. She would likely go out and celebrate. All this is as it should be for she would have just experienced a big, big win.

It would not be surprising if we found out that she also had a bit of trepidation. After all this would be her first CD. Will it be well received? Will it sell?

Now, imagine Elton John being contracted to produce another CD. I suspect his response would be quite different than our young singer-songwriter. Rather than getting high off the experience, it is very likely he remains quite sober. Rather than celebrate, it is likely he begins to plan. And do you think he wonders about his ability to produce a high quality CD that will sell? As it pertains to creating and producing music, I imagine Elton John is quite *Confident*.

Confident people share two important characteristics: 1- they know they will deal successfully with whatever life throws at them, and 2- they base their confidence in their innate abilities, rather than circumstances.

Chapter 3

M.O.s 101: The Basics

First and foremost it is important to understand that Methods of Operation are just that, Methods of Operation. Mainly, the M.O. Scale is a scale of winning and losing.

M.O.s are filters through which we approach our worlds and pursue our goals. M.O.s do not speak to the quality of an individual, only how that individual perceives and interprets their perceptions, draws conclusions, makes decisions and takes actions. Individuals with high M.O.s are not necessarily better people than those with lower M.O.s, and people with lower M.O.s are not necessarily worse people than those with higher M.O.s.

We all know of wildly, materially successful individuals who seemingly could care less for their fellow humans, who are happy to amass wealth regardless of how much destruction, pain, and suffering they leave in their wake. Similarly, we all know people who struggle from day to day to make ends meet and do what they can to help make the world a better place. There are awful people operating from every M.O. There are wonderful people operating from every M.O. There are people everywhere in between operating from every M.O. This is important to keep in mind as you read.

Remember, mainly, the M.O. Scale is a scale of winning and losing.

Basic and Specific M.O.s

We all have a number of M.O.s and they fall into two categories: Basic M.O.s and Specific M.O.s. A person's Basic M.O. is their general approach to the world. It is their approach as they do their day to day lives. You likely know people who just seem to worry much of the time. If one aspect of their life is going well, they talk about the areas of their life that are causing them concern. Their Basic M.O. would be *Failing*. You also likely know people for whom life is hard, no matter how easy they seem to have it. More often than not they are involved in a fight or struggle of some kind. Their Basic M.O. would be *Rebelling* or *Determined* depending upon whether they are struggling against obstacles or for goals. And of course you likely know people who seem to accomplish a lot and are generally and genuinely happy. Their Basic M.O. would be *Successful*.

Specific M.O.s refer to our methods of operation for specific activities. For instance, there are people for whom making money is an incredibly easy thing to do; you give them $1000 and they'll turn it into $2000. You can bet they have a very high M.O. regarding such endeavors. Sometimes some of these very same people might be seriously dysfunctional in some other aspect of their life. Perhaps they have had three, four, or even five marriages all of which have ended in divorce. Their approach, their M.O., at least as it pertains to marriage, is low on the M.O. scale.

Once established, Basic M.O.s tend to be quite stable. Specific M.O.s are more subject to change as individuals move from activity to activity; from areas of greater competence to areas of lesser competence and back again.

How M.O.s are Established

How do we come by our M.O.s? Our M.O.s, both Basic and Specific, are primarily a function of how much stress and success we have experienced in our lives. The equation is very straightforward: the greater the stress, the lower the M.O., the greater the success, the higher the M.O.

$$\uparrow \text{Stress} = \downarrow \text{M.O}$$
$$\uparrow \text{Success} = \uparrow \text{M.O}$$

Please understand that for the most part we are not aware of or responsible for our M.O.s – that is until we know we can choose them and learn how to do so. They are established subconsciously, below our awareness through interactions with our family, friends, community, our society at large, and the world we live in.

Parents

As very young children our parents and the type of home-life they create for us matters greatly. Initially a child's M.O.s are greatly influenced by those of their parents. If a mother experienced significant stress during her pregnancy, we now know some of the biological impacts this stress can have on her child's development, and those impacts can be quite debilitating. At the same time, given that the mother is under stress, her M.O. likely falls on the lower half of the scale. And if both parents experience a lot of stress, the likelihood of the child experiencing stress also is great, so increasing the probability of the child developing lower M.O.s on the problem-oriented half on the Scale.

Conversely, if during her pregnancy the mother is happy and for the most part at ease, and the child is born into a relaxed and successful environment, this increases the likelihood the child will feel productive and happy, and develop a goal-oriented M.O.s.

A number of years ago I went on vacation and visited two of my very best friends. Both had two children of the same ages, four years old and two years old. I stayed with each friend for days. During that time I observed how both families lived. As coincidence would have it I ended up going to the zoo with each family. For the first family preparing to go was hectic, tense, and hurried, bordering on chaotic. Mom was yelling at dad, dad was getting frustrated, all in an effort to make sure the food was prepared, the diaper bag was in the car, everyone had sunscreen on, and everyone who needed to go to the bathroom had done so. At the time this family was operating from **Rebelling** or possibly **Determined.**

The second family was the antithesis of the first. Mom and dad easily and calmly prepared everything that was needed: food, clothing, diaper bag, sunscreen, and made sure everyone who needed to go to the bathroom had done so. At the time they were operating from *Conservative* or *Confident*. Now both families made it to the zoo and both families had a good time, yet the ways they approached this event were vastly different. Over the years I have found both experiences to be rather typical for each family.

Many years have past since those excursions to the zoo. Today all four kids are in college. All four are great young adults. They are caring, respectful, and kind. They are very successful students, and they excel at a number of their extracurricular interests. However, it is not surprising to me that two approach life with a fair amount of stress, while the other two for the most part are confident and happy.

Of course our siblings play their role also. If they are supportive and help make our lives more successful and enjoyable, they will have contributed to our establishment of higher M.O.s. The same can be said for grandparents, aunts, uncles, and cousins; all those who influenced us as we were growing. That being said, typically our parents play the most significant role in the development of our Methods of Operation.

Friends

Our families are certainly not the sole determiners of our approaches to the world. As we get older our friends, and those we hang out with, also play an important role. The groups we identify with will strengthen our already existing M.O.s and at times help us to establish new ones. Of course, the choice of groups we choose to engage with is strongly influenced by the M.O.s we are operating through at the time we were drawn to them.

Rarely do goal-oriented, happy teens choose to hang out with those who act sullen and nihilistic. Similarly, you do not often find unmotivated kids excelling at sports, music, or theater.

The Media

Another group of inputs that significantly impact our M.O.s are the media we choose to absorb. It works thusly: our M.O. at the time of our media choices will determine what we choose, and what we choose further reinforces that M.O. So, what we see is what we get, and what we get reinforces what we choose to see. This self-reinforcing cycle is true for each M.O.

The music we listen to, the news we pay attention to, the books and periodicals we read, the television and movies we watch all contribute to the formation and maintenance of our attitudes. If most of the music a person listens to deals with violence, loss, death, and nihilism they should not be surprised to find themselves behaving as if the world is not a particularly fun place. If the books and periodicals a person reads are predominantly about grim people and events, they should not be surprised to find themselves feeling depressed. If the preponderance of a person's television and movie viewing deals with dysfunctional people behaving dysfunctionally, they should not be surprised to find themselves taking a dim view of their fellow human. As they say in the world of computer programming, 'garbage in, garbage out.'

Some time ago my cousin, who was 15 at the time, told me he watched Pink Floyd's "The Wall" every day for a month. For those of you not familiar with the movie, it's filled with dark imagery set to the band's music. When I asked my cousin how this went, he told me he found himself feeling a little depressed. My young cousin said it was a really good experiment; he learned the impact of music and movies on his psyche. It is a good lesson for us all to learn.

Maintaining Our M.O.s

Once established, M.O.s are fairly self-maintaining. What we end up believing about the world and our place in it, who and what we ultimately engage with, focus upon, and are drawn to are in large part driven by our M.O.s. In this way the woman who believes hard work will bring success never considers that success might not be so hard, and so never sees all the opportunities for easy, big wins that present themselves to her regularly. The man who grew up in a family where his parents argued frequently often assumes that it is not only okay to argue with his partner, but expects to. His friends will likely watch in frustration as he passes over numerous cool, fun, easy-going prospective partners in an effort to find one with whom he can struggle.

In the same way the person who grew up in a family where resources were plentiful might come to believe that all it takes to make money is a good idea and a little focused attention. From an M.O. perspective when it comes to making money that person's Specific M.O. is at the very least Successful. It would not be surprising if that person considered people on the lower rungs of the socio-economic ladder to be simply lazy and unmotivated.

I have always enjoyed school and as luck would have it, academics came easily for me and I excelled as a student. I have always been confident in my scholastic abilities. Having a **Confident** M.O. regarding academics I never really understood why some people seemed to find school so difficult and challenging. Some years ago I was studying for my martial arts black belt. As

I neared my goal the physical aspects of my training became harder and harder; so much so that twice I went home after training and was so frustrated that I actually cried. One evening after class I spoke with my instructor about my frustrations. We were friends and knew each other well; he was aware of my academic skills and I was aware of his personal dislike of formal education. After hearing me out he smiled warmly and said,

"Dr. Klusky, now you know how many of us felt in school."

He went on to help me address my frustrations and I did achieve my goal. However that one lesson was perhaps the most significant lesson I learned in my five years of training with him. I am an educator and for the first time I had real empathy for those who did not find formal education easy. From that day forth I became a much, much better teacher.

The Language of M.O.s

Once again, our M.O.s govern what we perceive and how we respond; they greatly influence what we believe we are capable of and what goals we set for ourselves. They are reflected in our language.

Each M.O. has a language of its own, almost as if each M.O. were a separate country. The languages of two M.O.s are more easily understood when the M.O.s are in close proximity to each other on the scale. The farther two M.O.s are from each other, the greater the difficulty will be in understanding. People operating from two highly disparate M.O.s might as well be speaking foreign languages. Let's look at two scenarios.

Have you ever been really angry about something and have a cheerful friend suggest you, "Turn that frown upside down," or some such insipid platitude? Perhaps they tried to encourage you to simply look on the bright side. If you are like me, I bet you were thinking, "You just don't understand!" They were not speaking the language of your Specific M.O. at that time. You were **Rebelling** and they were **Successful**, maybe even **Confident**.

Perhaps you've had a friend who believed they were seriously stuck in a situation and was very worried. Wanting to help, you saw a number of options for them and proceeded to give them some very workable ideas. To each of your ideas they responded with something like, "Oh, I couldn't do that," or "That won't work," and with each response came a "reason" why your idea was not a good one. Sound familiar? In this scenario your friend was likely **Failing** and you were probably Interested or **Successful**. In either case both parties were not speaking the same language and those who were trying to help had little success.

If you want to have greater success with others it would be to your advantage to be able to communicate from many different M.O.s. Remember, *people coming from M.O.s that are close to each other on the Scale can understand each other better than people coming from M.O.s that are farther apart.*

So, in the first scenario if the person trying to cheer you up would have begun by joining you in getting angry, you would more likely have identified them as your ally. Then, if they helped you focus your attention on a goal, they would have encouraged you to get **Determined**. From there you would have had a much better chance of success.

The second scenario would likely have required more work on your part. Starting with them at **Failing** you would have needed to guide them through to **Rebelling** then into **Determined**.

Let's take an example. Say your friend was very worried about not being able to complete a project on time and this worry was compounded by his fear of losing his job. You might try something like this: "I know it would be awful if you lost your job over this project. Your boss is being so unreasonable. What a jerk!" Now you are focusing his attention on his boss and your friend may begin to get angry. This is very good; he is moving up the M.O. Scale.

If you keep this up he will move up from *Failing* to *Rebelling* (being angry at his boss) and from there you can speak to him in the language of *Determined*: "What would it take to get that darn project done on time?" Once he starts to look for answers to that question he is now *Determined*. From there you can help him brainstorm. Now he will be more amenable to taking a look at your suggestions. You will then need to keep being *Determined* with him until he finds answers that will work.

Be careful at this point. As your friend continues up the Scale he will enter into *Careless* and have a tendency to want to "settle" for solutions that will not fully complete the project. If he stops here, soon after he applies one of the solutions he "settled" on, one that was "good enough," he can wind up back where he began: with an incomplete project and a dissatisfied boss.

So, when there are a number of potential ideas on the table, be *Interested* in how they might work and your friend will likely follow your lead and be Interested also. Keep focused until your friend has one or more solutions that will actually get the job done. In this way you have helped your friend move from a *Failing* approach to an *Interested* approach and you would have done him a great service.

If you are in sales, and we all are, you can see how valuable it is to communicate in the full range of M.O. languages. Whether you are selling a product to a client or selling a proposal to your boss, whether you are a parent selling the importance of education to your children or you are simply trying to sell your partner on a vacation destination, the better you can speak the M.O. language of your target audience the better chance you will have to succeed.

M.O.s, Trauma, and Resilience

Up to this point we have been discussing the establishment of M.O.s under the range of normal circumstances. What about more extreme conditions? Given that stress is one of the primary determinants of one's M.O., you can imagine the effects of experiencing severe trauma with its potential for overwhelming stress.

Now, people respond to event's in many different ways. An event that may traumatize one person may have little impact on the next. A person who is shot may, in rare cases, experience less stress than a person witnessing the shooting. Sometimes it takes only a single event to traumatize an individual. Other times it may take a series of events for an individual to be traumatized. Whether or not a person will be traumatized by an event depends on a host of factors. That person's M.O. is one of those factors.

The lower a person's M.O. is when they experience a potentially traumatic event, the more likely it is for that person to experience the event as stressful and be driven farther down the Scale. Additionally, that person will very likely take longer to recover. The opposite is true for a person operating from a higher M.O. at the time of such a potentially traumatic event. This person will be less likely to experience the event as stressful, and if they do, their M.O. will not be driven down as far. They are also likely to have a significantly shorter recovery time.

As of the writing of this book numerous American soldiers are returning home from Iraq and Afghanistan diagnosed with PTSD, Post Traumatic Stress Disorder. As capable, energetic, and gung-ho to do their duty as they were at the beginning of their tour, these soldiers are returning home much less so. It is a certainty that most, if not every one of these soldiers' M.O.s has deteriorated.

Many of these soldiers return home to wives and children, with their condition unaddressed. Some of these families remain intact; others split apart. Either way, the deteriorated M.O.s of these soldiers negatively affects the M.O.s of their spouses and offspring; often so much so that the M.O.s of those in their family also deteriorate. So now we have a child with a deteriorated M.O. who grows to be a man, raises a family of his own, and passes his deteriorated M.O. down to his children. This is one of the multi-generational effects of trauma.

Of course soldiers aren't the only ones experiencing trauma resulting in PTSD. Every day, around the world men, women, and children experience significant trauma as a result of abuse, poverty, war, and all manner of human rights violations. Almost all of them who are either raising or who will raise children will pass on the effects of their experiences to their succeeding generations.

Dr. Joy DeGruy, in her seminal book, *Post Traumatic Slave Syndrome: America's Legacy of Enduring Injury and Healing* demonstrates the effects of multi-generational trauma as it pertains to the African-American experience in America. It is an exceptionally clear presentation. In her work she poses the question: if one traumatic event, or a series of events, during a soldier's tour of duty can be powerful enough to result in a diagnosis of PTSD, what might the impacts of a lifetime of traumatic events be on an individual, their family, and their succeeding generations? One of the potential impacts of multi-generational trauma could be the passing down of chronically low M.O.s with the concomitant chronic dysfunctional approaches to life.

Yet it is clear that even in the face of such seeming hardship African Americans have been able maintain high M.O.s, demonstrating that the negative effects of multi-generational trauma are neither experienced, nor passed down the same way by all those at the receiving end. Some people, often those starting with higher M.O.s are more resilient and recover from such traumatic experiences on their own. Others have sought and received help, and so healed over time. Still others have taken the opportunity to chart a new course, and in the process make themselves even stronger than before, inculcating their children and grandchildren with their strength and wisdom.

Some families are so purposeful that the strength of their purpose protects them, and the force of their will drives them above and beyond their experience. At times children with an inner fortitude are born into impacted families. Their inner strength allows them to maintain their innate optimism; an optimism they then pass on to their progeny.

Within the pages of this book are suggestions and tools you can use to relieve stress, build resilience, and raise your M.O. Doing so you can establish new approaches that will fundamentally change how you and your family interact with the world.

Chapter 4

Knowing Thyself: Identifying M.O.s

What is your M.O.? What about that of your spouse? How about your business partner? Your boss? Your children? If you are going to take advantage of the M.O. Scale, you must first be able to identify M.O.s. You need to be able to identify your own M.O.s as well as the M.O.s of those with whom you interact.

Learning to identify M.O.s is a skill, and like any skill it will take practice to become competent. Once competent at identification, you will then be able to learn to move yourself up the Scale and choose your M.O. For now, first things first.

Identifying the M.O.s of Others:

When it comes to understanding what makes us tick we are often the last to know. It is typically much easier to know what's going on with those around us than with ourselves. After all, with greater distance comes greater objectivity. Nowhere is this more applicable than with learning to identify M.O.s. So, we will begin with learning how to identify the M.O.s of others, then move on to identifying your own M.O. Of course, everything in this discussion can be applied to identifying your own M.O. as well. Once again we must emphasize that until people become aware of them, they are not responsible for their M.O.s. Their M.O.s are unconsciously established as a result of the amount of stress and successes they have experienced.

The Big Three Indicators:
Attitudes, Emotions, and Behaviors

Remember each Method of Operation is comprised of three components: an attitude, an emotion, and a behavior. These all operate in conjunction with each other to make up a given M.O. Each component provides information to help us determine a person's M.O. To accurately identify a person's M.O. you need to take all three into account, and often you have to take them into account over time.

Attitudes

What is a person's attitude? What is their outlook on the world? Are they pessimistic or optimistic? Do they approach projects with trepidation or excitement? Are they worriers? Are they forward-looking? Do they tend to create problems or solve them? These are the types of questions you should ask yourself.

However, answering these questions alone will not necessarily allow you to accurately identify a person's M.O.

There are a number of people who have learned to 'act' up-beat and we give them credit for doing so, for acting upbeat can lead to actually being upbeat. That being said, acting successful and being *Successful* can be two very different things.

It is also important to consider that we all have bad days and good days. Over the course of our lives we will likely experience all the attitudes on the scale. Events occur producing certain responses in us; some of those events are of our own making, others we simply are the effect of.

Let's say you meet a man who seems to have a dim view of his world. You might identify his M.O. as *Failed*, and you might be right. But is this his *Basic M.O.?* Is this the way he regularly approaches the world? He may have just lost his job and this may account for his attitude. That night he may go home, lick his wounds, and begin planning his next move. Within two weeks he may have a better job at higher pay than his previous one. In this case his Basic M.O. is more likely *Successful*. To make an accurate assessment often requires information over time.

Emotions

Emotions are internal feedback of how we are doing on our goals; our needs and wants. If we believe we are losing, we will feel fear. If we believe our progress is being impeded, we will feel anger. If we feel we are advancing towards a goal we considering to be meaningful, we will feel happy. It is this connection between our feelings and our progress on our goals that makes our emotions such helpful indicators.

Most of us can label emotions quite readily. A person's emotional state can be a significant indicator of their M.O. However, simply identifying a person's emotional condition is not necessarily enough to determine their M.O. As with attitudes, most of us experience the full range of emotions over the course of our lives. It is a question of appropriateness and consistency.

A woman just finds out that her mother has cancer and is very worried. Is this a Failing M.O., simply appropriate emotion, or both? Four years after his cat died a man is still grieving the loss. Failed M.O., appropriate emotion, or both? A person just got that job they always wanted and is ecstatic. Successful M.O., appropriate emotion, or both?

While identifying a person's emotion at a given time can give us insight, it is not by itself usually sufficient to accurately identify their M.O. It is another story if you notice one of your employees typically is disgruntled and another of your employees seems content most of the time. When observed over time these can be very strong indicators.

Behaviors

Objectively observing behavior is where the rubber meets the road. A person's attitudes and emotions can tell us a lot; their behaviors tell us the most. What do they do? What effects do they produce?

The guy who seems happy, enthusiastic and communicative about his goal to be a musician yet who does not practice is likely **Undermining**, at least as it pertains to that particular goal. The woman who complains daily about all the work she has to do, yet somehow does it all well is more likely **Determined** rather than the undermining her complaining might lead you to believe.

If you watch a person operating from *Failing* you will see that person repeatedly make one or more mistakes that will keep him/her from succeeding. At the same time you will see them do just enough so they won't fail completely. If you watch a person operating from *Successful*, you will see them accomplish their goals with seeming ease. To the untrained eye they will sometimes appear lucky, but more often than not, if you look closely you will see how they created their apparent luck.

Reading Other Indicators

In addition to identifying attitudes and emotions, and observing behavior there are other indicators you can pay attention to in order to discern a person's M.O.

Listening to What People Say

Remember, each M.O. has its own language. Listening to what people talk about and the words they use can give you great insight into their Method of Operation. Do they talk about failures or successes? Do they talk about others' misfortunes and gloat over them? Do they express joy at the successes of others?

Do they hold themselves drearily silent, with little energy for speech at all? That would be *Lifeless*.

When they speak do they speak in *Defeated* terms? "That's impossible." "It's not worth trying, it will never work." "What's the use?"

Do they speak the language of *Failed?* "I'm not good enough." "I'm just bad at math." "I can't win."

Are they speaking *Failing*? "What happens if it doesn't work?" I'm afraid if I don't stop eating so many desserts I'll get diabetes." "Oh my God we may be attacked again."

Perhaps they are coming from **Undermining**. This one can be a bit tricky because it often looks like something else. **Undermining** is not so much what is said as how it is said. Backhanded compliments, propitiation, disingenuous or insincere efforts at pseudo-friendship all fall into this category.

They might be speaking the language of **Rebelling**.

"I hate _____!" "So-and-so pisses me off!" "I really need to lose this weight."

On the goal-oriented side of the scale, are they speaking **Determined?** "I'm going to get that raise if it kills me." "I'll show her, I'll get that project in on time." "You have to suffer to make success worthwhile."

Careless? "Whatever." "Don't worry about the details, let's just get it done." "We can get our work done later."

Interested? "Let's see how it works." "Not now, I'm working on a project." "Fascinating, how can I help?"

Do they speak **Successful?** "I just finished writing the final chapter of my book!" "Congratulations! You were wonderful!" "The workouts she was doing really improved her health."

How about **Conservative?** "Don't rock the boat." "Live within your means." "Quit on a win." "It's working, let's keep doing it that way."

Confident? Those who are confident speak with the certainty that comes with the experience of many successes. When they speak it is often with encouragement and enthusiasm. They expect to succeed and know things work will out to their advantage and the advantage of most of those involved. "Of course I/we can.

Observing People's Associates

Who people associate with makes a difference and says a lot about them. Typically, alligators marry alligators. Generally speaking, people will not associate for too long with others who are too different from themselves. It is just too uncomfortable. From an M.O. perspective, people operating from a particular M.O. tend to associate with others of the same M.O. or one close by on the Scale. This is why it is not uncommon for people operating from one of the lower M.O.s to ridicule the "Positive" attitudes of some of those operating from one of the higher M.O.s.

It is just as uncomfortable for people operating from higher M.O.s to hang out with those operating from lower ones. But, rather than focus on discomfort, their goal-orientation has them focused more on achievement. Lower M.O. interpretations don't occur to them or interest them once pointed out.

Organizations attract certain types of people, with certain M.O.s. The organizations that receive the highest ratings for employee satisfaction are most often those whose senior managers are at least **Interested** when it comes to interpersonal relationships. At the time I was doing my doctoral work at UCLA in the late 1980's the psychology department was known for its collegial environment. The students knew that as long as they put in a good and honest effort they would all be successful. My peers and I did whatever we could to help each other navigate the program. It was very much a win-win atmosphere.

During the same time the psychology department at Stanford had a very different reputation. In that department it was reputed that graduate students made their bones on the backs of their peers. It was supposedly a highly competitive win-lose environment. Seemingly the M.O. of Stanford's department was

Undermining. During my second year at UCLA a postgraduate student from Stanford joined the department.

Every Friday afternoon the psychology department at UCLA would host forums at which professors would present their research for discussion. Typically the discussions would center on proposing ideas for improvement and further research. I was surprised when the student from Stanford showed up to her first forum and proceeded to attack the presenter's work in an attempt to undermine it. I'm sure I wasn't the only one.

So, who do the people you know associate with? With whom do they surround themselves? Are their friends and associates working to improve themselves? Are they engaged in the world in some meaningful way? Are they enjoying their lives?

What People are Good At

Another useful indicator is observing what people are good at and what they are not. Typically, someone who excels at a particular activity has a high M.O. as it pertains to that activity. The opposite is typical when someone is incompetent. This is very straightforward. High M.O. → High likelihood of success.

Identifying Your Own M.O.s

Why should you spend time and energy to identify your own M.O.? First, it is simply a good idea to understand yourself. The more self-awareness you have, the better chance you have of becoming who and what you want to be. And though sometimes you might not be happy with what you learn about yourself, change is always possible.

So, second, and of greater import, your M.O.s are not etched in stone; they can be quite malleable. If you are going to choose the M.O.s that work best for you, you need to know where you are starting from to most efficiently change them.

Identifying one's own M.O. can be a little tricky at times. We are often the last to know about ourselves. Most of us also like to see ourselves in the best light, so it can make it somewhat more difficult to be objective. Be that as it may there are a number of approaches you can take to become aware of your own Methods of Operation. Of course the more honest and accurate you are willing to be regarding yourself, the simpler your task.

Identifying Your Specific M.O.

A good place to start is identifying some of your Specific M.O.s. Of the activities that you have put time into, which ones do you *not* do well? Which ones do you consider yourself to be *okay* at? Which ones are you *good* at? At which ones do you *excel*? How *unhappy* or *happy* are you with your involvement? Generally speaking the less capable you are, the worse your approach, and so the lower your M.O. The more capable you are, the better your approach, and so the higher your M.O.

Another way to examine your level of competency is to ask those questions from the perspective of your family and friends. So what would your friends say you're not good at, okay at, good at, and excellent at? One way to answer these questions is to simply imagine how your family and friends would respond. Another way is to go and ask them. Either way, you will have to take their M.O.s into account, as their M.O.s will color their assessments.

Once you have answers to these questions and get a feel for where you are on the scale as it pertains to each activity you can then explore how you approach these activities: What is your attitude towards the particular activity? How do you feel when you're doing it? What results do you typically get? Answer these questions and you will have a much better grasp of some of your Specific M.O.s.

Honing in on Your Basic M.O.

So how do you identify your Basic M.O.? How do you identify your basic approach to the world; the approach you unconsciously use most often? Start with examining yourself relative to the "Big Three" indicators: attitudes, emotions, and behaviors. What has been your usual attitude towards the world? Is your glass half empty or half full? Have you tended to be fearful or excited about the future? How quickly have you recovered your equilibrium from seeming setbacks? Have you been enjoying your life? What emotions do you typically experience? Do they tend towards the mercurial or more stable? Behaviorally, what types of results do you get? Do you accomplish what you set out to do? These are the types of questions that will give you strong clues as to your Basic M.O.

It is also very useful to look to your parents or those who raised you. What were their Basic M.O.s? This can be an excellent place to start. There is a fair likelihood that your Basic M.O. is close to that of those who brought you up. You can then look to the other people who have had a significant hand in your upbringing such as teachers, coaches and mentors.

Certainly consider what you talk about and listen with "fresh ears" for what language you use. Do you tend to be pessimistic or optimistic? Do you tend to discourage others or encourage others? When people leave your presence how do they feel? How do you respond upon hearing about the successes of others?

Who do you associate with? With whom do you surround yourself? What are your friends like? Are they working to improve themselves? Are they engaged in the world in some meaningful way? Are they enjoying their lives? When you spend time with your friends what do you do?

If you have a spouse or partner, what are they like? What's their M.O.? Are they having a good time? Are they advancing themselves in some way? Are they happy? What about your children? How do they move through their world?

What do you feed your mind with? What kind of movies do you enjoy? What television shows? What type of books interest you? What magazine articles do you read? What kind of games do you play? If you notice you fill your mind with a preponderance of stimuli from a particular M.O., it is a clue as to your own.

Finally, and most important, what do you think about yourself? How do you move through the world? Do you struggle? Do you worry? Do you find things interesting enough to learn something about them? Are you enjoying yourself? Are you happy? When you do things do they tend to come out right? Do you improve the lives of others?

These are the kinds of questions that can help you discover your own M.O. Answer these and you'll be well on your way to understanding a lot more about yourself. And if you're not satisfied with the answers, not to worry. There are many things you can do to raise your M.O.s and so be happier, more successful, and more fulfilled.

Choice

Imagine you are at a train station, and there are twelve trains about to leave for their destinations. Wouldn't it be beneficial to carefully consider where each train goes before boarding?

Each M.O. is like a train, carrying people along predictable routes to predictable destinations. The people on the train may engage in all manner of different activities, but regardless of how hard they may try, they are still on that same train, still heading for the same destination.

This is because M.O.s spring from the subconscious. Rarely, if ever, does one become conscious of the overruling aspect of the M.O. one is operating in. The M.O. is the powerful locomotive carrying us along its predetermined route.

Consider the plight of the businessman; so busy working IN his business that he never has time to work ON his business. He never has time to fix faulty systems, never has time to make the improvements he knows he should. So it is for each of us. We are so fundamentally guided by our subconscious M.O.s, so caught up in them, that we do not step back and notice the underlying trend in our lives; our M.O.

Fortunately, learning the M.O. Scale gives us an opportunity to step back and consider; to work ON our "business" instead of continuing to work IN it without real improvement.

Raising your MO will bring real improvements to your life. Improvements you can see, measure and build on. Thankfully, we can raise our awareness, discover our MOs, and choose to board a different train, a train of our choosing.

Chapter 5

Choosing Your M.O.: Moving Up the Scale

I first met Dr. Samuels in 1974 when I joined a group of students studying applied philosophy under his tutelage. In 1976, he began integrating his work in applied philosophy with business management theory. The M.O. Scale was one aspect of the coursework. Throughout the ensuing two years or so Dr. Samuels would point out the **_Undermining_** nature of some of my behaviors. I could not see it. I thought of myself as genuinely friendly, I rarely if ever spoke ill of anyone, either to their face or behind their backs. As far as I was concerned I was very helpful. I certainly did not think of myself as discontented. On the contrary I laughed a lot and believed myself to be upbeat.

Then, one day as I was discussing a book with him, I took it out to reference a particular section. To my utter surprise a letter he had asked me to mail for him two months before fell out. I finally saw the manner in which I undermined. This was but one event in a series of events over the preceding two years in which I "forgot", "spaced out," or otherwise failed to remember to do something I had agreed to do for him. In a flash I recalled six of these events, three of them actually costing him money. Seeing my realization show on my face, Dr. Samuels simply smiled. It was one of the most important lessons I have ever learned. I immediately went to work to change.

On the one hand our M.O.s are very stable subconscious constructs. Once established, our approaches to the world rarely change significantly throughout our lives. This is due to the fact that most of us remain relatively unaware of their existence. We are not typically presented with opportunities to examine ourselves in this light. It is this quality of stability that allows us to predict outcomes by looking through the lens of the M.O. Scale.

On the other hand M.O.s are not etched in stone. They can be changed. We can actually choose our Methods of Operation. If you recall, our M.O.s are primarily a function of the stresses that we have experienced and the successes we have had. Moving up the M.O. Scale then is a matter of reducing the stress and stressors in our life and increasing our successes. Doing both of these might be easier than you think.

When you change your Basic M.O. you change yourself in a very fundamental way. If you move up the scale far enough you will almost be a different person; you will see and respond to the world in a new way. You will notice you have different motivations than before. You will notice you are drawn to different types of art, literature, and recreational activities. You will even be drawn to different kinds of people.

It is important to differentiate between the M.O.s you may notice yourself operating from throughout a given day as you engage in a variety of activities (Specific M.O.s), and the raising of your Basic M.O. Specific M.O.s will change depending on what you are doing at any given time. You may be **Defeated** at noon as you study for a test and **Confident** at three o'clock as you prepare to present a proposal to the Board of Directors.

Basic M.O.s are far less mercurial; far more stable. To fundamentally and permanently change your Basic M.O. requires time. So please be patient with yourself and those around you seeking to make similar changes in their lives.

It is also important to note that when people move up the M.O. Scale they move *through* the M.O.s; they do not jump. As they move up the scale they adopt the M.O.s they are moving through. A person does not go from **Failing** straight to **Interested**. Individuals who have spent the better part of a lifetime being pessimistic and worrying do not usually become upbeat and focused overnight. To get to **Interested** from **Failing** they will spend some time at **Undermining**, **Rebelling**, **Determined**, and **Careless**, in that order, before they get to **Interested**.

It is important to note this because a person who has experienced and expressed fearfulness (Failing) as their dominant emotion will certainly experience and express anger (Rebelling and Determined) as their dominant emotion as they move up the scale. It is common to mistake this progression as an indicator that something is going wrong. On the contrary, something is going very right.

When we see a child who is very shy and quiet become angry and rebellious we often identify the new behavior as a problem. Sometimes we move quickly to stamp it out. On the face of it this can make sense; after all the angry, rebellious child can be a nuisance while the quiet, shy, acquiescent, inhibited child is quite manageable.

Looking at this child through the M.O. lens we see a very different story. This shy, quiet child (shyness being indicative of Failing) is growing more courageous. If the child is going to move up the scale to the goal-oriented M.O.s we know s/he will have to pass through **Undermining** and **Rebelling**. If we act to squash that undermining and rebelliousness in the usual way, with force, we will likely drive that child back down into quietly **Failing**. Instead, understanding the M.O. Scale, when that shy child starts acting out we see this as a step in the right direction and if we are skilled enough, encourage the child to focus his or her resentment and anger towards the accomplishment of a goal, and so help them move up through undermining, up through rebelling and finally become **Determined**.

Keeping this in mind, let's explore ways to move up the M.O Scale.

Reducing Stress Through Re-Ordering Our Lives

The less the stress, the higher the M.O. Too many of us experience far more stress than is necessary. Sometimes the stress we experience is a response to the pressures of the world around us – and our responses are governed by our M.O.s

Other times stress is a direct result of the way we have arranged our world. It is important to know that it is possible and important to arrange our lives to be easier, calmer, and more relaxed; to arrange our lives from a higher M.O.

Arranging Our Lives

There are a host of activities people pursue to reduce the stress in their lives. Meditation, prayer, alcohol, exercise, yoga, Tai Chi, sex, diet, music, drugs (recreational and prescriptive), relaxation exercises, and the list goes on. To be sure some of these, (drugs and alcohol) while providing short-term stress reduction, have the tendency to create greater stress down the road. Others (sex, music, etc.), while helping us take our minds off of our immediate situation, which has value in and of itself, do not often provide enough long-term benefit.

The best stress reducing activities are those that will not only make us feel better in the short-term, but will also make us spiritually, mentally, emotionally, and/or physically stronger, in the long-term. The more consistently we can engage in these types of activities, the more resilient we become and the better able we are at staying calm and relaxed.

Are we suggesting you go out, join a gym, hire a personal trainer, dietitian, and masseuse, sign up for yoga classes, and start interviewing spiritual counselors? Maybe, but remember, you're in it for the long haul. Start small and keep it simple. If you feel you are not getting enough exercise now, start by taking short walks during your lunch break. If you believe your diet is not as healthy as it could be, have a piece of fruit for dessert. Baby steps.

While we highly recommend almost all of the above, (drugs and alcohol being the exceptions) there is one activity that will do more to reduce stress than all of those combined:

Living Within Our Means

The great preponderance of stress we experience comes as a result of our efforts to be, do, and have more than our actual resources allow. And by resources we do not only mean money. Time and energy are also significant parts of the equation. In America far too many individuals, families, small businesses, and large corporations live beyond their means. Buying more things than we can afford, trying to squeeze 27 hours worth of living into a 24-hour day, expecting our workforce to do twice the work with half the manpower, all these activities and decisions result in greater stress. And the greater the stress, the lower our M.O.s and the less our ability to function.

So, if you want to reduce stress – live within your means. Financially, this is more possible than most people think. A few years ago a friend of ours rented the apartment in the upstairs of his home to a family of five who had just emigrated from Vietnam. Mother and father had three children ages twelve, nine, and seven. Both parents worked full time, minimum wage jobs. At the end of their first year they had saved $10,000! Within two years they had opened up a restaurant and a couple of years after that were able to get a mortgage on a small home. Of course they did not own a late-model car for quite a while, nor did they have cable television. Their children, while never dressed in the latest fashions, always had clean clothes to wear to school. They made it work.

Living within our means as it relates to time and energy is also quite possible. How many people do you know who habitually overbook themselves, filling up their schedules with activities they "must" do? There's always work to do at home, there are always social gatherings to attend, there's always some business to take care of, and my God all the driving we need to do to get our children to and from all their activities. There's just no time to rest. As a result they can't find time to sleep well, exercise, or eat properly – all of which increases stress.

With all there is to do, with our schedules as filled as they are, it is amazing how easy it is to drop almost everything when our child is involved in a serious accident or becomes deathly ill. It is amazing how little most everything else matters. The truth is most everything else has never really mattered much, we just thought it did.

So if you want to raise your M.O., just say no to lower priorities. Begin to develop the habit of leaving blank spaces on your calendar. Most of us can always find something to do; it seems harder to make time for nothing. It is so important to have free time, time to do whatever it is you feel like doing in the moment. Blank spaces on your calendar will certainly reduce stress. Blank spaces on your calendar will also give you time to help your friends and loved ones in emergencies. By the way, being of service in times of need will also add to your success quotient.

If parents try to do more than they can actually do, can the children be far behind? We know one high school student who was working to maintain a high average at school, training 15 to 20 hours a week as a gymnast, working and competing with his Math competition team, and playing an instrument in the school band, as well as taking care of his responsibilities around the house. He has been very successful at all of his activities. But at what cost? Is it any surprise that he is pretty stressed out a lot of the time? As he gets older and his approach becomes his habit, he is setting himself up for a stress-filled life, one in which his likelihood for happiness and fulfillment will diminish by the year. Worse still, he will probably pass this approach to living on to his children, should he have some. Being productive is great – to a point. Please help your children by making sure they too, have free time; time to rest, relax, and take in their world. It will serve them well.

It is also wise, and cost-effective, to encourage those around you to do the same. Businesses that overwork their employees, expect them to work 50, 60, and 70 hour work weeks, and routinely put unreasonable demands on them typically experience high turnover, many days lost to illness, and a less efficient workforce than they might otherwise have. Businesses that tend to have more stable, healthy, and happy employees are the ones that take their employees' time and energy resources into account, providing them with time throughout the day, week, and/or month to breath and recharge. As part of encouraging their employees to live within their means, these companies also care for the mental/emotional well-being of their people. Where possible they help their employees create schedules that work for them and their families, they provide opportunities to recreate, and they strive to make their workplaces enjoyable places to be.

Reducing Stress by Changing Our Responses

Stuff happens. Loved ones become ill, we lose jobs, sons and daughters go off to war, we are involved in automobile accidents, we get sick, a tornado or hurricane blows through our town. Some events are beyond our control. We cannot always choose what happens to us. But we can choose how we respond.

Imagine you are sitting with some people in a room when one of them has a heart attack. Some in the room might be paralyzed; others in the room might be stirred to action. Some might be traumatized; others not effected in any way. While it is unlikely that any of the people in the room consciously chose their response to the situation – they could have. Their responses are dictated by the M.O. they have regarding emergencies.

Stress and calm are learned responses. How we respond to a particular situation depends in large part on the M.O. we learned in response to similar situations. And our past stresses and successes in those similar conditions play a large role in determining our present M.O.

If we do not know how to help someone who is having a heart attack, and we have a history of **Failing** when we do not know what to do, we will likely default to that M.O. On the other hand, even if we do not know specifically how to help someone in such a condition, yet have a history of **Successfully** helping in emergencies, we will likely operate from that M.O. In this way our responses, for the most part, are left to accidentally learned M.O.s. The good news is, regardless of our history, we can choose to develop new responses – *intentional* M.O.s.

In the 1980s, there was a gentleman who was president of a highly successful insurance company who disciplined himself to respond, "That's great!" upon hearing seemingly bad news. He said he did this because it helped him look for solutions and keep his mind open to new opportunities. Among those who his company insured was Union Carbide. In 1984, Union Carbide's plant in Bhopal, India exploded killing thousands. You can imagine the look on the panicked employee's face when he delivered the horrific news, and his boss responded with, "That's great!" Did he really think this was good news? Of course not. He was mortified at the loss of life, but his response helped him keep his head while those around him were losing theirs.

So what will it be for you: Chance or Choice?

Our attitudes drive our behaviors which produce the consequences we experience. Think of A, B, C. Attitude → Behavior → Consequences. If you respond from an M.O. of **Failing** in particular situations and wish to develop a better M.O. and so experience different consequences, you can start by working to change your behavior. The president of the insurance company above trained himself through making a behavioral change. This worked for him.

Sometimes this is easier said than done. Sometimes behaviors do not change so readily. When behaviors do not change easily, you need a more powerful approach. *Working to change your attitude is that approach.* When your attitude changes, your behaviors will follow automatically. This is because changing your attitude will directly impact your M.O. There are a number of tools you can use to change your attitudes to ones that will serve you better. Here are two very simple and very effective exercises.

Use Your Imagination

Ask yourself, **"Are there aspects of my life that are not going well enough for me or that could use some improvement? If so, what are they?"**

Make sure you name and write down the areas. The answers are the areas where improving your attitude would help. Once you have identified an area ask yourself, **"What attitude would work best here?"** and explore different attitudes. Write your answers down.

Sometimes your exploration can be improved with a thesaurus and a dictionary. We often find we do not have the right label for the attitude we wish to adopt. A dictionary and thesaurus are great tools for expanding our attitudes vocabulary.

For example, let's say you get stressed out when you have to talk with your boss and you would like to develop a different response. You think the attitude you would rather take on is 'calm,' but this just doesn't quite hit it on the head. Go to your thesaurus and look up the word 'calm' and you will find a number of words that are similar yet not exactly the same. Perhaps 'peaceful' resonates with you more. Perhaps 'ease.' Perhaps 'serene,' 'relaxed,' 'tranquil,' 'still,' 'cool,' 'quiet,' or 'composed' better describes what you're after.

This exploration can be a lot fun; it can also be quite enlightening. When you find some words that might describe the state you are after, take the time to look them up in the dictionary. You'll get a deeper understanding of their meaning and a better feel for identifying which is the one that suits you best at this time. Make certain you write down what you learn from your efforts.

Once you have the word representing the attitude you want you can ask yourself, **"What would it be like to operate with this attitude?" "What would I be doing differently?" What would I look like if I was operating this way?** In this way you begin using your imagination to explore what your world would be like if you approached it from this attitude. As you explore you will notice your attitude beginning to change. The more full your exploration, the more your attitude will shift to the one you want. Imagine yourself going through your entire day with the attitude of your choice . . . then go out and do it. You may want to leave reminders for yourself on your refrigerator, in your bathroom, in your car, or on your desk – whatever you need to do to increase the likelihood of success. Do it and see what happens.

One time a number of us were sparring in our martial arts class. After we had gone at it for about 15 minutes Dr. Samuels stopped us and asked to us to imagine we were 900-year-old martial arts masters who had been successful in tens of thousands of engagements. He had us close our eyes and get the feel for what that would be like. Then he had us spar again. The difference was marked. We all became more still, more measured, and more direct in our attacks. We were all immediately better than we had been 10 minutes earlier. Results can come that quickly.

Memory Exercise (Samuels)

The *Memory Exercise* is a variation on the above approach and is quite simple. This exercise begins the same way, identifying an attitude or state you wish to create. This time instead of imagining what it would be like to operate from the state, simply, **"Remember a time you experienced (<u>fill in the state of your choice</u>.)"** Continue recalling times you experienced that state until your state improves.

Feel free to remember many different times you experienced the state of your choice or repeatedly remember the same one or two times you experienced the state of your choice. If you can't remember any, and this does happen once in a while, feel free to make some up. Your mind doesn't really know the difference. You may need to recall ten, twenty, or more individual events for your attitude to shift. Or you may need to remember the same event ten, twenty, or more times to get the shift you desire. More often than not though, it only takes a few repetitions.

SORTing™ and Re-Minding™

The above are very simple, effective approaches that work to give you control of your attitude. There are times though, when they are not enough. Sometimes one needs a bigger crowbar. If these exercises do not work well enough for you or your children, there are other, more potent exercises that will.

SORTing™ - Have you ever been bothered by an event in your life, thought about it for some time, then had that "Ah ha" moment, and really understood what was going on, let go of the bother and felt much, much better? That was your natural sorting ability at work. Have you ever been bothered by an event, thought about it for some time, and *not* come to that releasing understanding, only to have similar events continue to bind you in the future? SORTing™ is a tool that helps you reach those "Ah ha" moments, release the stress of those events, and greatly improve your natural sorting ability.

Re-Minding™ is a powerful tool that, through the use of strong imagery, allows you to literally reconstruct your mind. It is a remarkable technique for freeing yourself from unwanted thoughts and feelings so your natural creativity and energy are available to you. It's easy to learn, fun to practice, and wondrously effective. Both SORTing™ and Re-Minding™ are the work of Dr. Samuels. This is neither the time nor the place in which to explain these exercises and show you how they work, that would require two entire books. Fortunately, books on Re-Minding™ and SORTing™ are being written. If you're interested, please visit www.drjimsamuels.com.

Increasing Success

Reducing stress is one part of the equation. Increasing success is the other. Sometimes increasing success is as simple as noticing when you have been successful. We often do a whole lot throughout our day that we take for granted.

Dr. Klusky's Father

My father is an example. He was a good man. To me he was a great man. Oh, he never achieved any fame or notoriety; but his family, his friends and those he worked with knew the quality of person he was. He had a smile and a kind word for everyone he met; he would give you the shirt off his back. If upon entering your home he noticed your door squeaking, he'd look for a screwdriver and some WD-40 and fix it for you.

My dad raised three boys who all turned out to be good men, (I might be a little biased on this last point.) and took care of my mother, his wife of more than 40 years. Regretfully, my dad always believed he was lacking, that what he did was never good enough. You see, dad never made a lot of money and felt he didn't provide adequately for his family. However, by the time he retired he had saved enough money for him and my mother to live fairly comfortably through their remaining years.

In his mid-seventies, he contracted Parkinson's disease. Towards the end of his life he required around the clock care. Fortunately, he had the foresight and the means to be cared for at home. Unfortunately, towards the very end, this level of care was inadequate and he was going to have to go into a nursing home. My father knew that this option would eat away most of the retirement funds and leave my mother with precious little. So, instead of going into a nursing home, my father stopped eating, stopped drinking, and stopped taking any medication. He died on the holiest day of the Jewish year. Not bad for an Orthodox Jewish man. I hope he passed with an appreciation for how much he accomplished.

Simply being aware of all the good you do will increase the amount of successes in your tally, your success quotient. If you look upon your life and do not notice enough success, wake up every day with the intention of making your life or someone else's a little better. Think of little things you can do to improve the lives of your family. Think of little things you can do to make the lives of the people with whom you work just a little easier. Then do some of these.

Keep a log of who you helped and what you did. It's important that you should also enter all the successes you have had in pursuit of your own goals into your log. We guarantee you'll feel better and better about yourself as your tally rises. And as your success quotient climbs so will your attitude.

Do the same with your children. Help them notice all the good things they do every day. Teach them to plan to make their own and others' days a little better and teach them to keep track of all the help they provide. Of course, remember to give them plenty of hugs and kisses, praise and acknowledgment for the work they do to improve their part of world.

Provide them with opportunities to have many successes for themselves. Helping them set goals for themselves and helping them notice their accomplishments is a good way to help them build up their storehouse of wins and their self esteem. Speaking of wins, you can go a long way towards making sure they know how to find the wins in every game they play regardless of the outcome simply by asking them what went right, what they did well. Did they improve from the last time they played? Did they support their teammates? Did they have fun? That old adage still holds true: it really is not whether you win or lose; it is how you play the game. And if you play the game well, with the attitude you wish to exhibit . . . you win big!

The WINS Exercise (Samuels)

The more success we experience, the higher our M.O. becomes. The WINS exercise is designed to increase the number of our successes and our awareness of them. Additionally, this exercise takes advantage of the power of our imagination that we talked about on previous pages.

WINS is a most powerful exercise. If you and your family practice it on a consistent basis, we promise that your attitudes will improve and your odds for success will rise. Your children will become more self-confident and develop greater self-esteem. If this exercise is done diligently, over time you will become more and more aware of what you are actually capable of.

WINS is an acronym that represents the four questions that comprise the exercise:

W: What did you **W**in at yesterday?
I: What **I**mprovements could you make?
N: What and when would you like your **N**ext win(s) to be?
S: When you **S**ucceed, what **S**tate will you be in?
Feel that now.

This exercise works best if the answers to these questions are written down. We suggest you keep a journal to keep track of your progress. If you are doing this with your children, provide them with their own journal. It can be a fine diary or a simple spiral notebook. Any book that has contained, fixed pages will do. Basically, anything other than a three ring binder, in which the expectation is that you will add and remove pages, will do. Get together with your child and find something that they feel is cool to write in.

Title each page at the top: WINS, and make sure each page is dated. Start by writing down the WINS questions and use this as a reference. There is no need to write down all the questions on each page everyday. After just a few repetitions you will have learned the questions by heart.

Title and date the next page, write the letter **W** on the left side of the page, and answer the first question. After you have answered the first question go on to **I, N,** and **S.**

What did you Win at yesterday?

List everything you won at over the past twenty-four hours, everything that went well for you, everything you succeeded at, every person you helped, everything you did to make life a little better. Sometimes people doing this for the first time will have difficulty finding things to put on the list. That's just fine; it will get easier with practice.

What Improvements could you make?

Now is the time to notice how you could have made things go better. Did you make any mistakes? If so, how could you correct them? If something went well, how might you have improved upon your performance? Look over your day and make your list.

A word here about learning from our mistakes. Yes, learning from our mistakes can be a very good thing. However, a few years ago we heard Tiger Woods say something very interesting about this. Tiger was being interviewed after a round of golf in which he did not play up to his standards. The journalist asked him if there was something he had learned today from his mistakes? Tiger looked at the journalist somewhat quizzically and told him he never pays attention to his mistakes. He focuses on what he did right and works to do those things even better (to

64

improve). We found this to be a quite unique and wise point of view; something worthy of consideration. This approach has certainly served him well on the golf course where his M.O. is Confident.

What and when will your Next win(s) be?

Once you have finished listing your potential improvements you are ready to consider what you will be successful at today. List as many wins as you need to ensure a successful day. Sometimes all it takes is *one significant win* to make the day a rousing success. Sometimes it might take 10 or more. Most often somewhere between three and seven will do.

It is important to note that your Next Wins list is not your 'To Do' list. Often our 'To Do' lists are simply lists of tasks that hold little meaning for us. "Get kitty litter." "Take out the trash." "By a dessert for the potluck." Sure, we may "need" to get these tasks done, but completing them provides us with little sense of accomplishment. When you complete the items on your Next Wins list you should feel the sense of accomplishment you feel when you move closer to achieving a significant goal or fulfilling a meaningful purpose.

Use your list of improvements to help create your list of Next Wins. Mine various aspects of your life for potential successes: your physical health, career, family, friends, groups you belong to, your income and other material possessions, your education, intellectual pursuits, creativity, and your spiritual development. Once again, this could include anything you can do to contribute to your own goals and/or those of your family, friends, or community.

If you happen to be one of those types who usually have a 20 item 'To Do' list it, you might find it interesting to ask yourself,

"What is the most important thing I can accomplish today?" and limit your list to that one item.

That takes care of the "What" portion of the question. Now let's consider the "When" portion. Once you've listed your Next Wins the next step is to schedule them, to put them in time. Get out your calendar, day-timer, planner, or whatever you use, decide when you will get your Next wins done, and enter them in your organizer. We cannot emphasize enough how important this is. If you do not put your activities in time, the chances of accomplishing them go way down. Those who schedule their activities, have a much, much greater chance to succeed.

When you Succeed what State would you be in? Feel that now.

Finally, you need to consider what state you would be in, what attitude or outlook you will have, when you are successful. Once you have named that state, and optimally we are looking for a one or two word name, take a few minutes to feel it. Imagine what it would be like to be in that state throughout the day.

There is an old Chinese saying, "As in the beginning, so in the end." In our society we are repeatedly taught that events and things bring us states of being. "If I get that car, I'll be so happy." "When I get that raise I'll be on top of the world!" "If she agrees to go out with me, it will make my day!" This is generally our experience of life. This is the *effect* position and it is only part of the story, and the less important part at that.

There is also a *cause* position. If we take on the attitude and occupy the state we believe we will experience when we are successful at the beginning, before we engage, the chances of us being successful and ending up with the attitude we expect as the result of success go way, way up. So, if we begin as we expect we will end, our chances of ending up as we expect significantly increase.

By answering the question, *When you succeed, what state would you be in?* and feeling it at the beginning of the day, you can greatly increase your motivation and the likelihood the day will go your way.

As we said, WINS is an incredibly powerful tool. Imagine doing this every day for a month? How many wins do you think you would become aware of? How many successes over the course of the month might you create? How much pride and self-satisfaction might you experience? How many people might you help? What would it do to your attitude? Now imagine doing this for a year . . . five years . . . a decade . . . a life time. What might it be possible to accomplish? What quality of life might you create for yourself? How high might your M.O. rise?

Planning for Success

If few people have clear goals, even fewer have clear, workable plans. Go into any organization and ask, "What is your mission?" How many employees do you think will be able to answer accurately? How many different answers do you think you'll get? If you dig a little deeper and ask for the organization's goals, what do you think you'll find? If an employee knows the mission and the goals do you think s/he will know the organization's plans? You can go all the way up the ladder to the vice presidents, to the president herself, and we bet there would not be but a handful of people who can answer these questions the same way.

Now, every company we've worked and consulted for has had a mission statement. Heck, we helped to create some of them. The company's management team went on a weekend retreat to develop one. They also all have goals. They've had consultants come in and help develop them. We have been two of those consultants. Many even have plans for their goals' accomplishment. So what gives? It has been our experience that mission statements, goals, and plans wind up in someone's drawer or in some file on someone's computer never to be looked at again.

It certainly does not have to be this way. Here is an example of a company that take a different approach. Some years ago I was visiting my cousin in Colorado and went to his place of business. He is an optical engineer working for Ball Aerospace and Technologies, one of the engineering concerns at the top of the aerospace food chain. My cousin was part of the team that designed the mirror that replaced the original, faulty one on the Hubble Telescope. At the time of my visit he was working on a research satellite, "Deep Impact," whose mission it was to explore comets. By the way, it did so with much success in 2007.

As my cousin was taking me around the facility and showing me the spacecraft I saw, along a 20 foot wall of the main workspace, the *plans*. The plans were a color coded time-line specifying what needed to be done, when it needed to be done by, and who was responsible for each step. It struck me. that this was the first time I had seen a project's plans, any project's plans, up in a place for all to see. Talk about being on the same page! I thought back to all the organizations for which I had worked and consulted.

Having a clear goal sets the target. Having clear, workable plans lays down the path. Without a good plan, many endeavors are destined to fail. We have asked thousands of people if they have goals. About 85% come up with an answer, though most of them seem to be making something up on the spot. When we ask them how they will accomplish their goal, we almost always get blank faces. They don't know. Maybe 20% give us some generalized response. Of the 20% who have some idea, only about a quarter of them tell us in more specific terms. If we push further and ask if they have a written plan, we usually get nothing.

How can people expect themselves to be successful? It seems we spend some time encouraging each other to come up with goals. Not so much when it comes to drawing up plans for their accomplishment. One of the results of talking about goals without plans is that those goals are not really connected to the physical universe. Many folks are walking around thinking they have goals, not understanding they have nothing of the sort. If they do not connect their goals to the physical universe, through some kind of meaningful plan their 'goals' are not much more than wishes.

Even when people do have a plan, if they are not acting on that plan, they do not have a goal. Only when they are taking steps to accomplish the goals they set for themselves can we say the goal is genuine. So if you're going to take the time to develop workable plans, do your best to make sure you are planning for your true goals. Planning will be a lot more motivating.

There are many reasons plans are so important. First and foremost they enable us to see where we're going. They are the map that gets us from here to there. Plans also serve a motivational purpose. When our goals are significant and their accomplishments are far in the future, each step of our plan provides us with smaller goals, the accomplishing of which enable us to keep our motivation high. So if you would like to plan effectively here is an approach to insure all the basics are covered.

PLANS (Samuels)

>   **P:** Purpose and Goal
>   **L:** Logical Steps
>   **A:** Action Analysis
>   **N:** Numbered Steps
>   **S:** Schedule

For a plan to be workable it must have a clearly defined purpose and goal, a logic for its accomplishment, an analysis of the necessary actions that demonstrate the plan is worth doing, and numbered action steps, each of which are scheduled with appropriate target dates. Oh yes, one more thing: for a plan to be useful, it has to be written down.

Purpose and Goal

What's your goal? "I want to make more money." "To be happy." "I'm going to lose weight." "To run a marathon." "To be healthier." All good goals, yes? Not really. Actually, only one of the above is a goal, do you know which one?

Remember goals are *endpoints* that we are working to achieve. The more clearly defined and measurable the endpoint, the better the goal, and when I say 'better the goal' I mean the more likely it is to be accomplished.

Of the goal statements above only one refers to a clear end point . . . "To run a marathon." The others are not goals, they are purposes. Purposes and goals are different. *Purposes are directions, goals are endpoints.* 'Going east,' is a purpose, going to a particular city east of where you are, is a goal. To accomplish the purpose of going east all you have to do is take a single step towards the east and thus, your purpose is fulfilled. Accomplishing meaningful goals usually requires a little more.

You want to make more money? Here's a dollar. You're done. You want to be healthier? Here's a carrot. If you eat it, you will be a little healthier. *How much* money do you intend to make? What can you do that will indicate you have achieved a measure of health that satisfies you? You get the idea.

This being said, purposes are senior to goals, they should come first. Optimally our goals flow from our purposes. *Accomplishing a goal is more meaningful if it is linked to a higher purpose.* The purpose answers the question, "Why?" "Why do you want to run a marathon?" "I want to run a marathon so I can challenge myself and prove to myself that I can get in shape." "Why do you want a six-figure income?" "I want to be more at ease." "Why do you want to weigh 140 pounds?" "I want to weigh 140 pounds so I will feel better about myself." Your purpose is the answer.

There is another important aspect to consider when thinking about goals. A goal is an image that we are **working** toward accomplishing. This working aspect is critical. If a person is not working toward the accomplishment of their goal, what they are claiming is their goal actually is a want or a wish. In fact, if you want insight as to what a person's actual goals are, look at what they are, in fact, working on. You'll get a good look at their M.O.

Logical Steps

How are you going to go about accomplishing your goal? Does this make sense? If you follow this path will you likely get there? Do you need to be more specific? Your logic will give you insight into how well you understand what it is you need to do.

The more simple, straightforward, and complete your logic is, the more fully you understand the tasks ahead of you. Take all the time you need to work out the logical steps of reaching your goal. Keep checking to see if your logic will result in your goal's fulfillment. If you aren't certain how to proceed, learn from the example of others who have succeeded.

Action Analysis

Have you ever taken on a project that you came to learn was a mistake for you? You know, it was such a good idea, it was so exciting, doing it was a no-brainer. You didn't think too much about the cost or the amount of time it would take, it was not that hard and it was so, so worthwhile. Then you got into the project and realized it was going to cost four times as much as you thought and going to take three times as long. Halfway through you looked in the mirror and asked yourself, "What in God's name was I thinking?"

This has happened to everyone we know at least once. Some of us are a bit more hardheaded than others and experience this with some frequency. It's one thing when we do this in our home, spend a couple hundred or couple thousand more dollars than we expected, and ruin four weekends. It's another thing when corporations do it, lose millions of dollars and are forced to lay off hundreds of workers. It's still another when our government does it, costing us billions of dollars. At every level this is the result of poor, little, or no consideration for the true expense of a project. (Remember, "live within your means?")

Action analysis is that stage of planning where you consider, as accurately as you can, the costs associated with pursuing your goal. Only after you have a reasonable estimate of these costs can you decide whether or not the goal is worth it. In this stage of planning, applying your Logic, you create a list of all the steps you need to take to accomplish your goal, then for each step you figure out how much it will cost and how much time it will take to complete. This is called the ACT formula.

Action. Cost. Time. (Samuels)

When planning a project put three columns on a sheet of paper:

Action	Cost	Time

List the steps you have come up as you detail the logic of your approach and fill in the other two columns. Humans are notorious for underestimating the resources needed to accomplish their goals, especially when it's something they really want. So, when you are evaluating your actions in an arena that is relatively new to you it's a good idea to multiply the costs and time by a factor of three, as these pursuits have a tendency to require three times the money and time than we originally allot. As you get more experience in an area you can reduce this to a factor of two.

When you are finished not only will you have a better idea of how much your endeavor will cost and how much time it will take, you will also be able to evaluate if there is something better you can do with that money and time.

Numbering the Steps

Assuming the action analysis turned out favorably, that is you've decided it is worth it to pursue this goal, the next phase of planning requires that you arrange all the steps in order and number them. This gives you another chance to make sure everything is accounted for and in its proper place. *Your first drafts will almost never be correct.* You will think of things that need to be added in the middle or rearranged. So, let your first draft be messy, with lots of added notes, lines, and arrows. Number the steps, and re-number them until it finally makes sense.

Then write up your actual plan, knowing that once you actually begin working it, you'll probably need to revise it continuously.

Scheduling

The final phase in planning is fantastically important and often overlooked. Scheduling each step of your plan is how your plan interfaces with the physical universe. Time management specialists understand that if something isn't scheduled, and they mean recorded in some kind of planner, the probability of it getting done goes way down. If you write your tasks down or record them in some way, the chances of them being accomplished go up significantly.

One more thing: In addition to having your plans in a file on your computer or in a journal . . .

Put your goals and plans in clear sight!

There you have it. When most people in the world, for all intents and purposes, are leaving their lives to chance, those who are willing and able to direct their lives are the ones who will likely have the most success and do the most good.

The better you plan, the greater your chances for success. A good plan also increases the likelihood that you will notice your successes as you progress toward your goals. And, of course, the more successes you notice and appreciate, the higher your M.O. will climb.

Conclusion

Looking Through the M.O. Lens

M.O.s matter. How we perceive and approach the world matters in every endeavor in which we engage. Whether you are putting together a team for a project, exploring a romantic relationship, or building a family, attitudes, frames of mind, M.O.s matter. Having learned through experience, many of us naturally take these into account, but still many others do not.

In the summer and fall of 1914, Ernest Shackleton put together his crew for what would turn out to be one of the truly great stories of survival and rescue. For those of you unfamiliar with the tale, Shackleton sought to lead the first team of explorers to trek across the Antarctic continent. He never made it. His ship, the Endurance, was trapped and crushed in the Antarctic ice leaving him and his men to fend for themselves for what was to be 21 months. After surviving almost a year and a half, with no hope of rescue, Shackleton, his navigator Frank Worsley, and four others set out to cross 800 miles of the world's roughest and coldest seas in a 22 foot life-boat, making for a whaling outpost on South Georgia Island, a tiny speck of an island in the South Atlantic. After spending 17 days in that life-boat they finally arrived, on the wrong side of the island. They would have to trek 30 more miles to the outpost, being the first people to cross the 10,000 ft. mountain chain that ran down the spine of the island for good measure. Three months later, after being forced to wait out the worst of the Antarctic winter; he was able to bring his men to safety. Perhaps most amazingly, all 28 men who began the journey made it home.

As Shackleton interviewed prospective sailors for this adventure there was one quality he prized above all: *a sense of humor.* You see, he had been in the Antarctic twice before and knew even under the best of conditions how rigorous such a journey would be. He had learned from his experiences that his team's attitude, their frame of mind, would be what would count the most, especially when the going got tough.

In the mid-1990s, the Portland Trail Blazers began assembling one of the most talented teams in NBA history, a team that in a few years would be infamously known as the Jail Blazers. By the 2000-2001season nine players on their roster had been all-stars. That team was unceremoniously bounced out of the first round of the playoffs. During that season when issues of team chemistry were brought up to the general manager, he famously said he, "never studied chemistry in college." By 2003, they were out of the playoff picture and attendance had declined precipitously as fans left in droves. In 2008, under the leadership of a new general manager, the Trail Blazers began putting a team together focusing on attitude as well as talent. In 2009, they were back in the playoffs with a team their fans loved.

Another way of saying this is that people matter. Who they are, their motivations and goals, their families, their world view, their "intangible" qualities, all matter. How many times have we seen organizations large and small behave as if their employees are simply a cog in a machine; if one breaks, just replace it with another? And how many times have management in these organizations been surprised when things go awry; when one employee sows the seeds of discontent and another turns out to be a thief? On the other hand there are those organizations that understand the primacy of the individual and give appropriate consideration to the individual's "intangible" qualities.

The more insight we can have into a person's "intangible" qualities the better choices we can make as to how best to relate with them. Looking through the lens of the M.O. Scale can help provide these insights. The M.O. lens not only can explain past behavior, it can also be used to predict the likely outcomes of future interactions.

Looking through the lens of the M.O. Scale can serve us in many ways. In romance there is great value in identifying the M.O.s of the object of one's affection. Likewise, there is great value in identifying the M.O.s of the parents and other significant family members involved. Understand the M.O.s in play and you will get a good sense for how a relationship might play out. They say that love is blind, and in many instances this certainly seems to be the case. However, in a society with a 51% divorce rate and where many of those who remain married believe themselves to be unfulfilled, it would seem at the very least prudent to enter into serious romantic relationships with our eyes as wide open as possible. The M.O. Scale can help you open your eyes.

For those who do have life-partners, the lens of the M.O. Scale illuminates ways to strengthen and deepen the bonds of love. For as a couple's M.O. rises so does their capacity for enjoyment and fulfillment.

For parents perhaps the greatest gift you can bestow upon your children is that of a high M.O. A high M.O. is the closest thing there is to a guarantee that your children will be able to create the rich, rewarding, and fulfilling lives you dream for them. Of course, the most significant step parents can take towards this end is making sure their own M.O.s are on the goal-oriented side of the Scale. Fortunately, regardless of your starting point, it is possible to raise your M.O. to any level you choose.

In business understanding the M.O. Scale can help with hiring and promotion decisions. Such understanding can also provide insight into team dynamics as well as office politics. Facility with the Scale can help sales and marketing personal refine their approaches to their audiences. It goes without saying that understanding M.O.s can give one great advantage during negotiations.

Looking through the M.O. lens can inform so much. From business relationships to friendships, romantic partnerships to family dynamics, looking at interactions through the lens of the M.O. Scale has provided people insights that have allowed them to successfully navigate the sea of human interaction. Perhaps of greatest import, understanding the M.O. Scale has provided people with a blueprint for changing their lives. May it do so for you and yours.

Appendices:

A.   M.O. Identification Checklist

B.   Steps for Raising Your M.O.

C.   Contributing to Raising the M.O.s of Others

M.O. Identification Checklist

Below is a checklist of questions to consider when identifying M.O.s.

Identifying the M.O.s of Others

- What results are they consistently producing?
- What attitude are they typically projecting?
- What emotions are they frequently expressing?
- What do they talk about and what M.O. language are they generally speaking?
- Do they tend to be more pessimistic or optimistic?
- Do they tend to be more discouraging or encouraging?
- Are they enjoying their lives?
- What are the M.O.s of the individuals and groups with whom they associate?
- What TV shows to they watch, movies do they enjoy, literature do they read?
- How do you usually feel after spending time with them?

Identifying Your Own M.O.

In addition to considering the questions above for yourself, you should also consider the following:
- What are the M.O.s of your parents' and/or those who have had a significant hand in raising you??
- What are the M.O.s of your siblings?
- What is the M.O. of your spouse/partner?
- If you have children, what are their M.O.s?

Steps for Raising Your M.O.

Reduce Stress

Arrange Your Life Accordingly

- Live within your means: financial, time, and energy
- Attend to your physical health: diet, exercise
- Attend to your mental/emotional well-being: relax, make
  time for yourself
- Attend to your spiritual well-being

Develop the Responses You Wish

- Use your imagination (pg. 57)
- Memory Exercise (pg. 59)

Increase Success

- Engage in activities on a daily basis that improve your life as
  well as those of your family, friends, and community, and
  make sure you acknowledge your successes. WINS (pg. 63)
- Take the time to plan for the fulfillment of your purposes and
  the accomplishment of your goals. PLANS (pg. 70)

Contributing to Raising the M.O.s of Others

Whether we are talking about a family member, small group, sub-culture, culture, our nation, or humanity as a whole there are steps we can take to contribute to the raising of M.O.s.

Prerequisites:

1. Ensure that your own M.O. is sufficiently high on the Scale
2. Maintain your M.O.
3. Decide if you truly want to engage with and support the individual or group. If so . . .

Reducing Stress

- Smile
- In general communicate in the languages of the upper M.O.s. (do not engage in gossip , undermining talk, or other communication using languages from the lower half of the M.O. Scale)
- Communicate from the M.O. above the one they are currently operating from if they are not at Successful or above.
- Support those in leadership who motivate from the higher M.O.s. (Remove your support from those who motivate by fear, conflict, or other M.O.s lower on the Scale.)
- Support those in the group who articulate positive, proactive, forward-looking visions.

Increasing Success

- Be aware of the group's goals.
- Help them plan and encourage them to move forward.
- Acknowledge and validate the successes of others.

Index

About the Authors

Dr. James R. Samuels

Dr. James Samuels, began helping others improve their memories as a teenager in 1962. He has spent the succeeding 48 years developing and refining his applied philosophical approach to human development. His development of SORTing™ in 1975, introduced a robust set of techniques lay individuals could use to release life-times of previously unresolved stress, and greatly increase their understanding and self-awareness.

Soon after, he turned his attention to the world of business integrating mnemonic training with a strategic approach to planning and management. In the 1990's, he adapted his work in applied philosophy to found The Principles of Engagement, a Martial Arts system and trained Andrew Gainer a 3-time world champion.

Dr. Samuels has been a prolific innovator/educator, working with thousands of people, providing them with tools to relieve stress and fulfill their potential. Today his work has culminated with Re-Minding™, a truly extraordinary blend of SORTing™ and mnemonics that allows people to free themselves from unwanted thoughts and feelings and release their natural creativity and energy. It is a major therapeutic breakthrough in self-management and personal freedom.

About the Authors

Dr. Jay Klusky

Dr. Jay Klusky received his Ph.D. in Cognitive Psychology from UCLA in 1990, under the guidance of Dr. Allen Parducci. Two years later he published his first book, *"Easy A's: Winning the School Game."* In 1974, he began his studies in applied philosophy under the tutelage of Dr. James Samuels, studies which he continues to this day.

Dr. Klusky has lectured at universities, developed and administered alternative high schools for youth considered at-risk, designed programming for those considered talented and gifted, and taught classes for students of all ages. His work culminated in his most recent book: *"What Every Parent Wants for Their Child and How to Get It."* Currently he serves as a mentor/life-coach/academic adviser, helping parents prepare their children for life after high school and helping teens develop the skills necessary to have extraordinary lives.

For more information regarding his work please feel free to visit his website. www.jayklusky.com

Coming soon by Dr. Samuels

Re-Mind Yourself

Re-Minding™ is a remarkable technique for rapidly freeing yourself from unwanted thoughts and feelings so your natural creativity and energy are available to you. It is a major breakthrough destined to enhance the practice of many forms of therapy. You can use this powerful tool for self-management and expanding your personal freedom.

Re-Minding™ will not only improve your memory, it will free you from unwanted inhibitions, conflicts, hostilities, sufferings and confusions.

Re-Minding™
Volume I

Re-Mind
Yourself

James R. Samuels, Ph.D.

More, it will help you clarify what you really want in your life and bring your natural powers of concentration and confidence to a new high and focus.

Change your mind – Change your life!

Re-Mind Yourself is scheduled for release by the end of 2010.
To order your copy go to:
www.drjimsamuels.com

Also by Dr. Klusky

What Every Parent Wants for Their Child and How to Get It

As the world rapidly changes, so do the demands placed on your children. If they are to meet these demands and enjoy inspired lives they must be ready. Today the old school rules no longer apply. The 3 R's, while still important, no longer guarantee entry into the middle-class. The college degree, once so coveted, only gets a foot in the door. Learn what you can do to prepare your sons and daughters to meet today's challenges, and create rich and rewarding lives.

Dr. Jay Klusky presents a well articulated point of view on a much needed discussion about the education and parenting of children. This is not a bland reiteration of data and statistics regarding "best practices" for working with children and youth. This book is a brilliant and remarkable critique of today's young people, their needs and challenges. Dr. Klusky takes us on an important and personal journey about how to successfully raise children to be healthy, productive and contributing human beings. This is a book that we can all truly benefit from reading!
Joy A. DeGruy, PhD

To order your copy go to:
www.jayklusky.com

Also by Dr. Klusky

Easy A's: Winning the School Game

I have enjoyed working with Dr. Klusky for almost two decades. His book is the best book I have ever read on how to study successfully. It's easy to read and apply. The success of my students is testimony to its effectiveness.

Karen Abrams, Founder,
Upgrade Academic Coaching

I've known Dr. Klusky for over 30 years, which is all his scholastic life. I always wondered how he did so well in school with so little apparent effort. After reading *Easy A's* I am pleased that he has been able to set down his methods in a concise, thoroughly readable, and clear blueprint for others to follow.

Gilbert Witte, M.D.

"Easy A's: Winning the School Game" was written for students and speaks directly to them. It is a most accessible and fun read, filled with great tools to help students study, organize, and strategize for college. Like all his work, the focus is on students taking responsibility for their own lives and education.

To order your copy go to:
www.jayklusky.com

The M.O. Scale

(Dr. James Samuels)

	M.O./Attitude	Emotion	Behavior
Goal-Oriented ↑	+6 Confident	Certainty	Knows
	+5 Conservative	Contentment	Maintains
	+4 Successful	Happiness	Wins
	+3 Interested	Curiosity	Focuses
	+2 Careless	Boredom	Unfocuses
	+1 Determined	Anger	Strikes out (for)
Problem-Oriented ↓	-1 Rebelling	Anger	Strikes out (against)
	-2 Undermining	Resentment	Destabilizes
	-3 Failing	Fear	Causes Losing
	-4 Failed	Grief	Causes Loss
	-5 Defeated	Apathy	No Desires
	-6 Lifeless	Hopelessness	No Future